BLUE and WHITE

The Cotton Embroideries
of Rural China

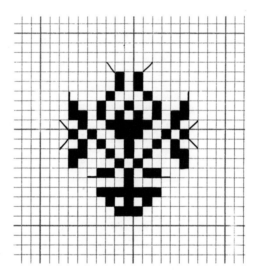

Chinese theater party

BLUE and WHITE

*The Cotton Embroideries
of Rural China*

by Muriel Baker and Margaret Lunt

Charles Scribner's Sons / New York

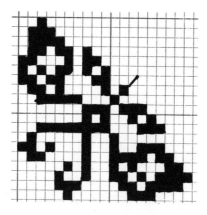

"Birds Singing at Dusk" reprinted by permission of Peter Pauper Press, Inc.

Excerpts from *Roving Through Southern China* by Harry A. Franck, reprinted by permission of Hawthorn Books Inc., copyright 1925 by The Century Co., all rights reserved.

All pictures from the Field Museum of Natural History by Ron Testa, Head Photographer.

Copyright © 1977 Muriel L. Baker and Margaret Lunt

Library of Congress Cataloging in Publication Data

Baker, Muriel L.
 Blue and white: the cotton embroideries of rural China.
 Bibliography: p. 102
 1. Embroidery—China. 2. Folk art—China.
I. Lunt, Margaret, joint author. II. Title.
NK9283.A1B34   746.4′4   76-57933
ISBN 0-684-14887-0

1 3 5 7 9 11 13 15 17 19 MD/C 20 18 16 14 12 10 8 6 4 2

Printed in the United States of America

ACKNOWLEDGMENTS

The largest share of our indebtedness goes to Dr. Bennet Bronson, Assistant Curator, Asian Archaeology and Ethnology, at the Field Museum of Natural History in Chicago. Without his enthusiasm for our project and without his many kindnesses this book could never have been written. We were allowed to read and to draw upon the late Dr. Carl Schuster's unpublished material on this subject and to study and photograph the hundreds of examples Dr. Schuster collected while traveling in China in the 1930s.

The late Miranda Packard's notes and examples were invaluable as they supplied a different point of view.

To the following for permission to use pictures and material we are grateful: The Field Museum of Natural History, Chicago, Illinois; Museum of Fine Arts, Boston, Massachusetts; Hawthorn Books, Inc., New York, N.Y.; Peter Pauper Press, Inc., Mount Vernon, N.Y.; The Textile Museum, Washington, D.C.

Our sincere thanks to our photographers, Harold Pratt, Marion Lewis and Ron Testa, for such beautiful pictures.

To Heather Clark, Bernice Gagne, Virginia Morrissey and Barbara Sargent Valenti, who spent many long hours patiently charting the intricate designs, not only our thanks, but our admiration.

And we thank Elinor Parker, our editor, who so graciously guided us. She's the best!

MURIEL BAKER
MARGARET LUNT

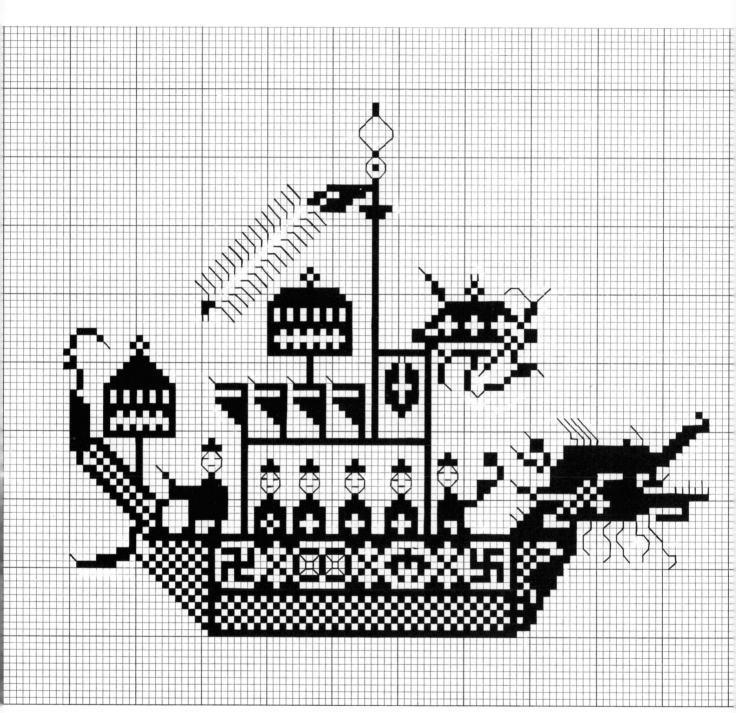

A dragon boat similar to the ones shown on Plate 8

INTRODUCTION

I am honored to be asked to introduce the book of Muriel Baker and Margaret Lunt. They have presented their unique subject with genuine insight. They have brought to their work a perspective all too rare in the study of Asian arts, that of the artist-craftsman already expert in the skills involved. And they have chosen to study an Asian art as important as it is little known. The beauty and intricacy of the folk embroideries of western China will come as a revelation to all their readers, including many of those who thought they already were familiar with Oriental textiles and needlework.

The majority of the embroideries described in this book were collected in the 1930s by Dr. Carl Schuster. It may therefore be useful to give some background on both Dr. Schuster and the collection he made.

Dr. Schuster himself was an interesting man, a generalist who knew China rather than a specialized Sinologist, who by the time of his death in 1969 had acquired an international reputation. As one of Schuster's mentors, the great Austrian anthropologist Robert van Heine-Geldern, put it, "In his particular field, the study of symbolic folk art, he had no equal."

We should remember, however, that "the study of symbolic folk art," as Heine-Geldern understood the phrase, was already becoming unfashionable among scholars by the time Schuster started collecting embroideries in western China. The theory had been worked out by a group of anthropologists at the University of Vienna, Schuster's alma mater—if one could collect a large enough repertory of authentic folk motifs from an isolated (and so, unspoiled) part of the world, one could discover in that repertory symbols that had been handed down from ancient times. One could then compare these with similarly ancient symbols in other places and thus uncover evidence of early migrations of peoples and other ancient cultural phenomena.

In order to carry out this program, Schuster chose western China as a suitably isolated and unspoiled area and decided that embroidered textiles offered the best local source of folk motifs. He was fortunate in his choice. He had happened on one of the world's great unknown traditions of folk design and managed to recover many examples of it just as it was on the point of disappearing. But without question the future of his studies and the nature of his collection were both affected by what he had originally set out to do.

The arguments against the Vienna theory are many and complex and need not be related here. The important fact is that Schuster remained loyal to the theory long after almost everyone else had rejected it, and this meant that he was isolated from his anthropological colleagues during the later decades of his life. Since his anthropological training meant that he was already isolated from his other potential allies, the Sinologist–art historians, he became an academic lone wolf in later years. As a result, his work and the embroideries themselves were never as well known as they deserved to be.

Schuster's theories had other effects as well. The need for a large repertory led him to collect a great many specimens, a much larger number than is usually included in museum collections of a single kind of artifact from a single place. This makes his collection extremely valuable for many purposes, including some that Schuster himself did not foresee. On the other hand, the idea that the motifs were survivals of an ancient system of symbols led Schuster to pay less attention than we might wish to nuances of symbolic meaning as understood by the people who made and used those particular textiles.

This criticism, however, should not be allowed to detract from what Schuster did. He first set out for the field in 1932 after three years of studying Chinese in Peking. He made, in all, four trips into western China, concentrating on Szechwan, Yunnan and neighboring parts of other provinces: a first trip in 1932, a second from August 1935 to January 1936, a third from July to September 1936 and a fourth from October 1937 to March 1938. During this comparatively short time, although often forced to travel on foot through dangerous areas and in spite of time-wasting bureaucratic complications, he succeeded in assembling a carefully annotated collection of almost two thousand specimens. These represented an art that was then unknown to the outside world and that is in fact still known almost entirely through pieces Schuster collected.

Upon his return to the United States in 1939 Schuster began the massive job of cataloguing and photographing. He published several articles on the subject and held two public exhibitions in New York, at Holland House in 1942 and at Asia Institute in 1948. These efforts attracted some attention from students of Oriental art and of needlework, but not enough to bring him financial support for publication of his projected masterwork, a complete illustrated catalogue of the collection.

He began to disperse his collection in the late 1940s, although he naturally retained notes and photographs on each specimen. A number of pieces were sold or given to individuals. Some were sold to various museums, both here and abroad. However, the great bulk of Schuster's collection was eventually lodged in two repositories. In 1952 the Museum für Völkerkunde in Basel, Switzerland, purchased most of the specimens, perhaps five hundred in number, which Schuster knew to have been made by minority or tribal peoples in southwestern China, Laos and Vietnam. And in 1960 the Field Museum of Natural History bought the rest of the collection, almost one thousand pieces possibly or definitely of Han Chinese manufacture.

The Field Museum's purchase initiated a warm friendship between Schuster and the staff of that institution, including the then Curator of Asian Ethnology, Dr. Kenneth Starr. This led eventually to Schuster's decision to give the museum his extensive files of notes and photographs. In combination with the collection itself these form a unique resource for the study of Chinese folk textiles and embroidery.

The resource is only now beginning to be used as widely as it deserves, and this particular book represents the first important result of such use. One hopes that it will in turn lead to other books and articles, perhaps one of them the comprehensive catalogue of which Schuster dreamed. One does not expect, however, that many of those books and articles will be written by persons with the professional dedication and charm of the present authors. We at Field Museum have greatly enjoyed working with them. We wish them and their book every success.

11 July 1976   Dr. Bennet Bronson
                                   Assistant Curator of Asian Ethnology
                                   Field Museum of Natural History

HSIU

Chinese symbol for embroidery HSIU

The cool wind of evening
Blows bird-song to the window
Where a maiden sits.
She is embroidering bright flowers
On a piece of silk.

Her head is raised
Her work falls through her fingers
Her thoughts have flown to him
Who is away.

A bird can easily find its mate
Among the leaves,
But all a maiden's tears
Falling like rain from Heaven,
Will not bring back
Her distant lover.

She bends again to her embroidery,
I will weave a little verse
Among these flowers of his robe . . .
Perhaps he will read it
And come back again.

THIS POEM, written by Li Po, the great Chinese poet of the T'ang Dynasty (618–906), is an introduction to China, a nation with so old a civilization that it is hard to realize just how far back in time it goes. China's recorded history dates from 841 B.C. in the Chou Dynasty, while myths and legends record the first stirrings of ancient man centuries before that.

CHINESE DYNASTIES

Historical periods in China are divided according to dynasties:

Legendary Period

Emperor Fu Hai

Shen Nung

The Yellow Emperor

Yao

Shun

The Hsia Dynasty	1990–1557 B.C.
Shang Dynasty	1557–1050 B.C.
Chou Dynasty	1050–221 B.C.
Early Chou	1050–722 B.C.

841 B.C.—history accurately dated from here on

Spring and Autumn	722–481 B.C.
Confucius	551–479 B.C.
Warring States	481–221 B.C.
The Ch'in Dynasty	221–207 B.C.
The Great Wall built	
The Han Dynasty	206 B.C.–220 A.D.
The Three Kingdoms	221–265 A.D.
The Western Tsin Dynasty	265–317 A.D.
North and South Empires	317–589 A.D.
The Sui Dynasty	589–618 A.D.
The T'ang Dynasty	618–906 A.D.
The Golden Age of the Arts	
The Five Dynasties	906–960 A.D.
The Sung Dynasty	960–1127 A.D.
The Partition	1127–1279 A.D.
Yuan Dynasty of the Great Kublai Khan	1280–1368 A.D.
Marco Polo visited China	
The Ming Dynasty	1368–1644 A.D.
The Manchu Dynasty	1644–1911 A.D.
Boxer Rebellion—foreigners expelled from China	
The Chinese Republic	1912–1949 A.D.
The People's Republic of China	1949–

The four great Chinese dynasties are considered to be the Han, T'ang, Sung and Ming. It was during these periods that the Chinese made incredible advances in all facets of their culture.

CHINESE ARTS AND CRAFTS

One thousand years before 356 B.C. when Alexander the Great was born, the Chinese had a written language. They were weaving, making pottery, casting bronze and carving jade, and they had needles for sewing and embroidery. In Sian, Shensi Province, some six thousand years ago in a Neolithic culture, the Chinese were using bone needles of all sizes, even down to a few inches. They had a calendar and they understood the principles of astronomy. They had invented printing and as early as 1005 A.D. had published an encyclopedia which covered all subjects within the knowledge of man at that time. It is recorded that even during the earliest of times the men were skilled carpenters and the women were clever at weaving and at needlework.

Scholars have called the T'ang period the greatest period of creative art in China. The Chinese themselves refer to it as the "Golden Age." The first T'ang emperor was Li Yuan and the second was T'ai-tuong. In 712 the greatest of them all, Hsuan-tsung, came to power. In the forty-two years of his reign all the arts and crafts flourished. There was a clearly marked distinction between arts and crafts, and it is an interesting one—painting, poetry and calligraphy were considered arts, and all the rest were crafts.

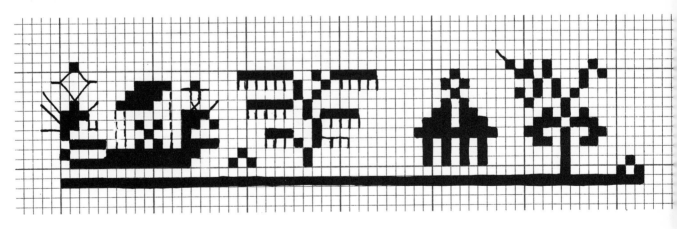

It was during this time that there was a great migration of foreigners into China. Persians, Arabs, travelers from India and Greece came to this faraway country over the romantic silk trade routes. Many found homes and were happily employed. Many left their imprint on Chinese arts and crafts of the time, having brought with them inspiration from their own native craftsmen. Persia, in particular, seems to have had a very strong influence, and many Chinese textiles seem to have motifs closely related to Persian-Sassanian textiles of 226–637 A.D. This is true of the beautiful silk embroideries, the magnificent mandarin coats and the glorious wall hangings that everyone thinks of when Chinese embroidery is mentioned.

THE COUNTRY EMBROIDERIES

It is also true of the small part of Chinese art that students of Chinese culture have entirely overlooked—the country embroideries, the art expression of the Chinese people themselves, of the rural millions. This enormous segment of the population was spiritually isolated from the rest of China. The people were ignorant in the

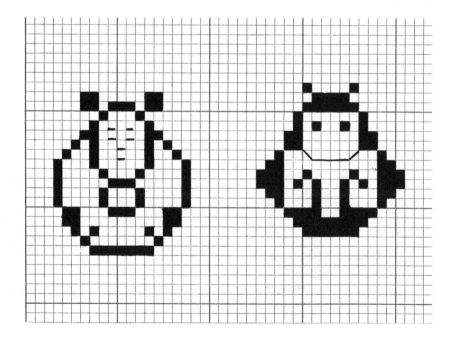

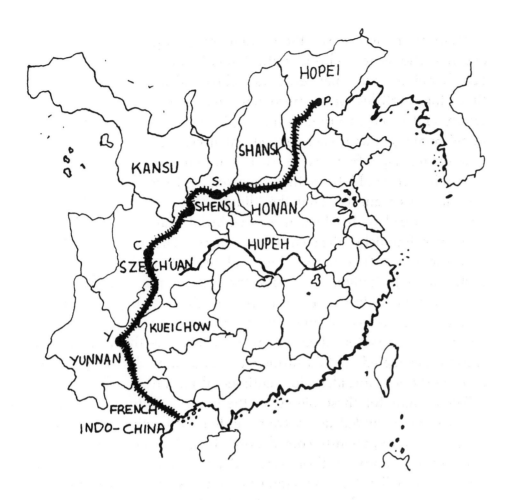

Map of Dr. Schuster's 1932 journey into the interior of China.
Many of his embroideries were collected there.

sense that they had no sophistication. But they had many traditions and customs, a culture of their own. They were of the earth, and their art shows their harmony with nature; peace and serenity are its essence.

These blue and white embroideries are found, for the most part, in the country homes and in the small villages nestled in the mountains of China's remote provinces. They seemed to have been especially popular in Szechwan, Shensi and Yunnan Provinces, although specimens have been found in Kweichow, Hunan and Hopeh Provinces as well.

5

Many years ago it was the custom for young ladies of prosperous households to embroider the "linen" for their future homes: door hangings, bed valances, pillow slips and mirror covers. Sometimes these articles were embroidered by the older members of the family and given as presents, many times on the occasion of marriage. Some of them, such as bed valances, were used only at the time of marriage. Some were used then and took their place in the everyday household from that time on; still others were reserved for the use of guests. That the "linen" was a coarse cotton cloth and the thread with which it was embroidered was also of cotton in no way diminishes the charm of the pieces. The cotton background was a lovely, soft, creamy white and the cotton thread was dyed dark blue with indigo. As a class, the bed valances show the finest work, and the oldest of these pieces are the best in technique and design. This art was dying out forty years ago and in all probability has completely died out by now, because the younger generation considered it "old-fashioned," and only the older women kept pieces of embroidery for sentimental reasons.

The designs for these pieces, in the highest traditions of decorative art, were handed down from mother to daughter. For generations they were patiently copied, stitch by stitch. Dr. Carl Schuster, who made a study of these embroideries while he was in China, says, "We shall not be far wrong in picturing to ourselves many of these same motifs being copied by daughters and granddaughters two, three, five or more centuries ago and with very little difference from their modern appearances."

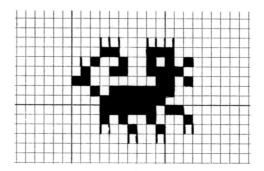

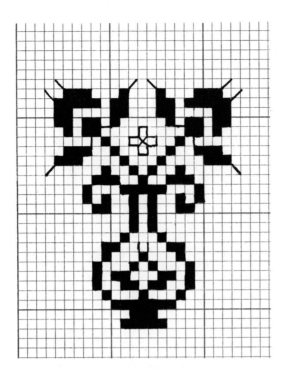

The designs are always entertaining and many times they are real masterpieces. Because of the structure of the Chinese language, the opportunities for punning are endless in the motifs of these embroideries. Many depict China's myths, some tell a complete story, some are no more than beautifully worked designs.

Some of the finest, most elaborate designs come from Szechwan Province, where they appear on bed valances and the embroidered borders of bed sheets. These sheets are three strips of plain cotton cloth sewed together. A fourth strip, elaborately embroidered, is sewed to the edge of the plain sheet and hangs down over the side of the bed so that it can be seen at all times. This strip is about 6 feet long and 12 inches wide and is densely embroidered with medallions, 12 inches in diameter. It is within these medallions that the puns, myths and stories are revealed.

The embroidery was also used on clothing: caps, jackets, pockets, aprons and the sash ends of men's clothing. The small caps worn by children were often elaborately worked as were sleeve bands, ankle bands, trouser legs of outer wear, children's bibs and collars.

DESIGNS

In this age-old art are motifs that date back to the T'ang Dynasty (618–906 A.D.) and even beyond. Some motifs show a foreign influence. How did it seep down into these remote hills and valleys, many accessible only on foot? Harry Franck in his delightful book *Roving Through Southern China* describes a day's journey through Szechwan Province in this fashion:

> Monday . . . proved to be the hardest day of the overland journey, if not indeed the hardest day of travel I ever saw in China. I thought the road and the weather had already done their worst, but it rained almost all day, now in downpours, less often a mere drizzle, though the morning was clear and the noonday, hot. The trail was from the very edge of the town an unbroken succession of rocks and stones, long ago thrown together into

what the Chinese mistake for a road and with mud between them in which my horse slipped and stumbled and my coolies did far worse. To say that the road was belly-deep in liquid mud is to give only a hint of how indescribably atrocious it was. To make matters worse, we ran into and soon became inextricably tangled up for all the rest of the trip with a caravan of about two thousand pack animals and horses, mainly loaded with opium, with chair-borne officials, merchants, families and the like without end. . . .

All morning we struggled along a small river by a mud trail beyond description, and all afternoon high above a smaller stream coming down through a great gorge, too narrow to pass anyone struggling from the opposite direction, of whom luckily there were few, and with at least a thousand places to go sliding to destruction. . . .

Dr. Schuster, who made many of these arduous journeys and who collected many of the cotton embroideries pictured here, says, "There are striking resemblances between some of these embroideries with the medallions designs, and the well known silk fabrics of Sassanian Persia which show similar medallions." In fact, it seems as if some of these motifs may have been imported from Persia specifically for this purpose.

These inherited designs varied from locality to locality and from family to family. There were countless minor variations, because millions of peasant women practiced the art. That a domestic tradition of this sort could flourish for untold generations implies a long period of political peace and isolation from external influence. This accounts for the fact that the art was not modified to any extent, despite minor variants; the tradition was so firmly established that it could not easily be deflected or changed. Also, the very cheapness of the material safeguarded the tradition. No great emphasis was placed on originality, but rather on the worker's ability to copy accurately in order to ensure the purity of the traditional designs. Even small variations made by a gifted worker would to a large extent be neutralized by the overwhelming traditionalism of the community. The designs were very closely copied; thus there is very little deterioration of style in them. Some were bold, some delicate, yet they were similar in general character. They were not the work of trained designers, but rather an expression of the people, who took great pride in them. These designs, untampered with and passed down as a whole, preserved for those who follow, are pure folk art.

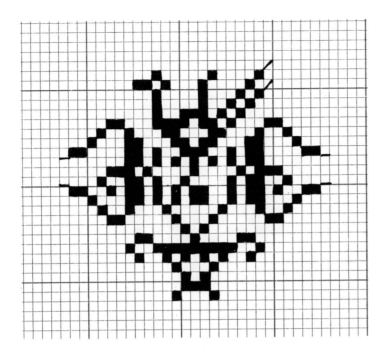

These embroideries represent the taste of the people, made by loving hands for their own use. *The designs have not been found elsewhere in any kind of Chinese art.* They come as a great surprise to those who are used to the decorative arts of the rest of China. To them the embroideries seem wild, strange and almost "un-Chinese" despite their beauty and elegance. Yet they show a great affinity to folk art the world over. Like all folk art objects, they were never cherished, no value was placed on them, and when a piece was worn, it was copied and the fragments of the original were either discarded or were utilized in making children's clothing. Dr. Schuster, in his voluminous notes, writes that "a sympathetic observer of these designs will feel at once in them a power of imagination which places them in a class by themselves."

Working the embroidery was not a pleasant pastime for its maker; rather it was a necessity, a labor of love, a real part of her life. And just as myth, story and symbolism were an ingrained part of her life, so these are shown in her designs.

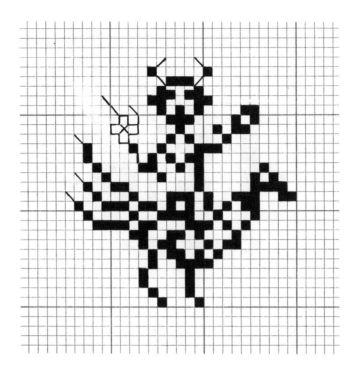

Lady Alford in *Needlework As Art* says, "Symbolism in Art is what metaphor is in speech. It is the representation to the eye of an object which suggests something else besides itself."

Often symbolism is used to tell a story or to get the message across to those who cannot read. The Chinese are extremely sensitive in the field of symbolism, and this sensitivity helped to create the exquisite designs of Chinese art.

As we have said, the Chinese rural folk were of the earth, they identified with it, it was part of their very being, it bred in them a vivid imagination, an imagination that fed upon the symbolism of ancient folklore. This folklore found expression in the work of their hands.

Perhaps the best known, certainly one of the oldest, of all the Chinese symbols is the so-called Yin-Yang. This charm is used throughout China to counteract evil. It is found over the door of most country homes, the one-story houses of simple architecture, with thatched roofs of straw and walls of beaten clay, of cornstalks

12

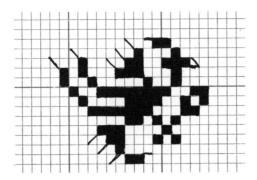

tied together, of bamboo strips woven together and plastered with clay, possibly whitewashed. In this charm, the circle represents the universe. The Yin and the Yang are the male and female principles of creation. The Yin, the female element, represents the earth. The Yang, the male element, represents heaven, the sun and light.

Yin-Yang symbol

Throughout Chinese folklore runs the theme of the Immortals.

Chang Kuo-lao: usually pictured riding backward on a donkey with the peach of immortality in his hand.

Han Hsing Tau: always has a basket filled with either fruit or flowers.

Lan Ts'ai-ho: plays his flute through endless time.

Li T'ich Kuai: is a cripple. He has a staff and a gourd on his back.

Chung-li-chu'an: is bearded. He usually carries a fan and sometimes a peach.

Lu Tung-pin: has a sword with magical powers and a fly swatter.

Ho-Hsien-Ku: is the only woman Immortal. A peach and a lotus are her symbols.

Ts'ao Kuo Chiu: does kindly deeds and carries two tablets of wisdom.

The Immortals are often pictured in the medallions on the embroideries of the country people. They played a real and vivid part in their everyday lives and therefore were often used as design inspirations. They were old friends.

Although we often find Chung Ku'ei depicted in the arts, he is not to be confused with the Immortals. He nevertheless possessed magic, the kind of magic that could drive away evil spirits. Clad in rags, he hides his ugly face with a fan.

The Chinese believe that there are Five Blessings. Different sources list them differently. One set is Longevity, Happiness, Peace, Virtue and Wealth; another, Longevity, Wealth, Health, Virtue and a Natural Death.

The Coins

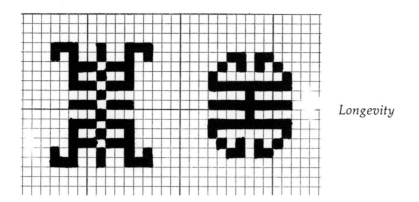

Longevity

There are Eight Precious Things: Dignity, Wealth, Married Happiness, Harmony, Charms against Evil, Charms against Fire, Personal Charm and Happiness. All these are identified by symbols such as the happiness symbol.

These symbols are found throughout the embroideries, some hidden inconspicuously in the border and corner pieces, others placed more prominently in the piece of work.

The Five Evil Creatures, or the Five Poisons (*Wu-tu*), are the snake, the three-legged toad, the scorpion, the spider and the centipede. Sometimes they are identified as the three-legged toad, the scorpion, the salamander, the frog and the snake. Separately, they are all to be feared. Placed together, they may ward off evil. The five poisonous creatures are often embroidered on children's bibs as a talisman, in which case there is usually a tiger in the center of the group as a sort of counter-talisman! The three-legged toad inhabits

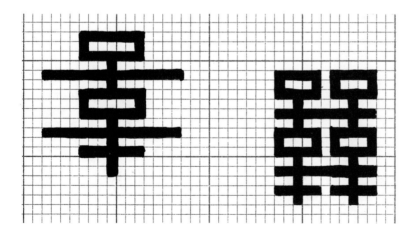

Left: Happiness
Right: Double Happiness

15

the moon. It belonged to Liu Hai, a nineteenth-century minister of state who was well versed in magic, and acted as his horse. Unfortunately, it had a way of escaping and going down the nearest well. It could be retrieved only by fishing for it with a string of golden coins.

There would be no Chinese symbolism without the dragon. This wonderful creature that symbolizes power in all its forms is the genius of goodness and strength and is the very fiber of life itself.

Although the dragon does appear to belong to the most conservative kernel of this country art, we sometimes find a pair of dragons fighting for a pearl: this is an emblem of great antiquity.

Again, we find the great dragon-gate, supposedly localized at the rapids of that name in the Yellow River, through which, in the third moon of the year, the carp make an ascent. Those that succeed in passing the rapids are turned into dragons. This idea is applied to successful graduation, a literary examination, a successful career, many children. In most instances there is a child within the gates.

The dragon is a good symbol, a kindly creature who had nine sons; these sons are found protecting various things. The River Dragon guards rivers and bridges, the Fighter Dragon is found on swords. There is a personal dragon who watches over you and your household. The five-clawed dragon is the Imperial Dragon and denotes supreme power. The dragon is all-inclusive.

Dragon

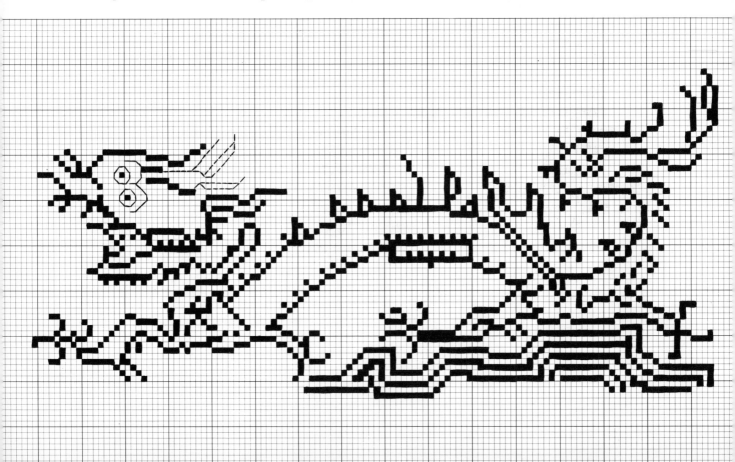

He unfolds himself in the storm clouds,
He washes his mane in the blackness of the
  seething whirlpools,
His claws are in the fork of the lightning,
His scales begin to glisten in the back of
  the rain-swept pine trees.
His voice is heard in the hurricane, which
  scattering the withered leaves of the forest,
Quickens a new Spring.

The bat has a most important role in Chinese folklore. Loved by most, it represents happiness and long life. It is much used in the embroideries, sometimes so elaborately delineated that it nearly becomes a butterfly! When used as a design in groups of five, it is a pictorial rebus that stands for the Five Blessings. The Chinese name for the bat (flittermouse) is *fu*, which also happens to be the sound of the written character meaning happiness. So at a very early date the rebus-writing of a bat was used to indicate happiness.

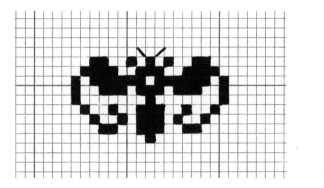

Bat

Another favorite symbol of the embroideress was the butterfly, the symbol of joy, brightness, summer and the soul. It might also be called the Chinese Cupid because it also signified true love. It is depicted in many forms and many ways. Butterflies' wings are sometimes embroidered in a solid dark mass, spotted all over with tiny rosettes like stars, suggestive of the night sky. Used in a border, the butterfly is directed alternately upward and downward within the curves of a vine. When the butterfly appears with the cat or with melons we undoubtedly have a rebus—the illustration of a pun.

17

Butterfly

Two birds, the phoenix and the crane, are celebrated in Chinese legends. The phoenix is the emperor of all birds and the sign of peace and prosperity, while the crane denotes longevity, old age and immortality. The popular and often-used phoenix comes in many varieties. The various interpretations produce a sort of bird par excellence—THE BIRD. This is no particular bird, however. It is always and invariably designated by the one term, phoenix. It is always represented somehow in flight. It is usually drawn with a head like that of a cock, with characteristic comb and beak and in most cases a protruding tuft of feathers about the neck. The tail feathers resemble those of a pheasant. Sometimes it is shown with a hanging head, as if it were dead.

Small birds are usually perched on branches. If a ship should happen to be part of the design, the birds are shown flying near the masts.

18

Phoenix

The domestic cock is also usually perched in a tree. Sometimes he has a rider on his back—intended as a humorous touch.

Ducks often have lozenge rosettes ornamenting their bodies. This seems to have set them apart, marking them as birds of special significance.

In eastern Szechwan, the crane was used to symbolize long life and often helps to identify fabric origin.

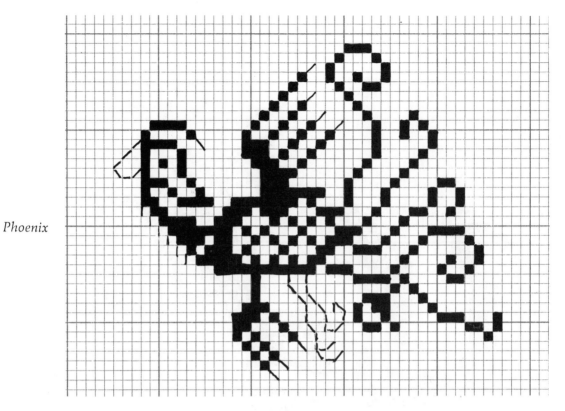

Phoenix

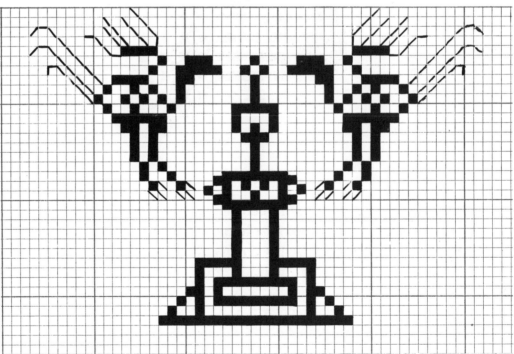

*Stylized motif with conventionalized birds from
an old sampler found near Tsonhua*

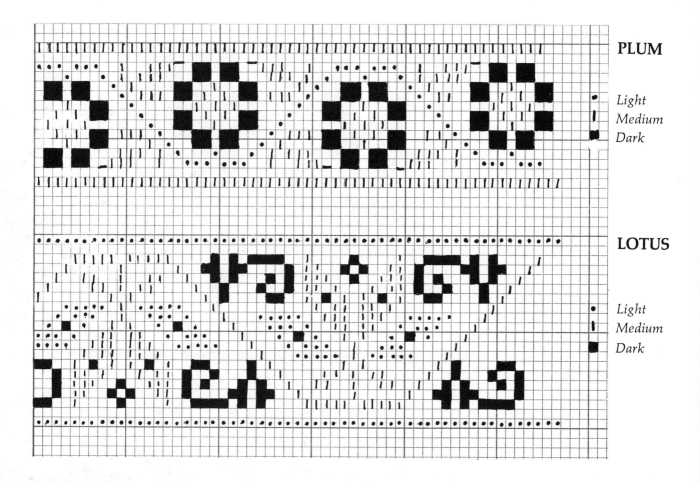

PLUM

Light
Medium
Dark

LOTUS

Light
Medium
Dark

BORDER DESIGNS—THE TSONHUA SAMPLER

In the town of Tsonhua, Hopei Province, in the late 1800s two marvelous samplers of border designs were collected by Miranda Packard, a nurse at a medical mission there. Women coming to her dispensary embroidered for her, while awaiting their turn, borders copied from the clothing that they wore, which recorded ancient designs.

There was the plum, the emblem of winter and the symbol of long life; the sacred lotus, emblem of summer and symbol of fruitfulness; the peach, emblem of marriage and the symbol of immortality and spring. The Chinese peach is different from ours in shape, having a well-defined point, which is always emphasized in the design. The peach is often used in association with the swastika.

21

Four o'Clock Bud

Peach and Bat

Borders from the Tsonhua sampler

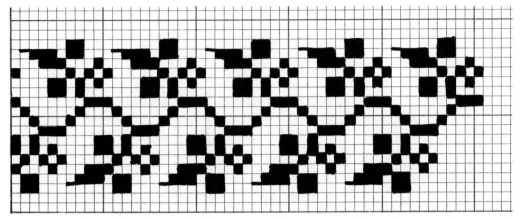

Leaf

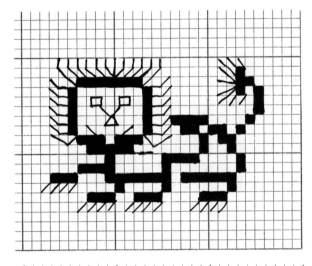

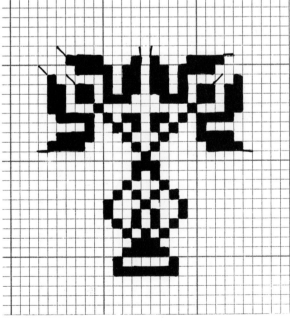

Small figures from the Tsonhua sampler

23

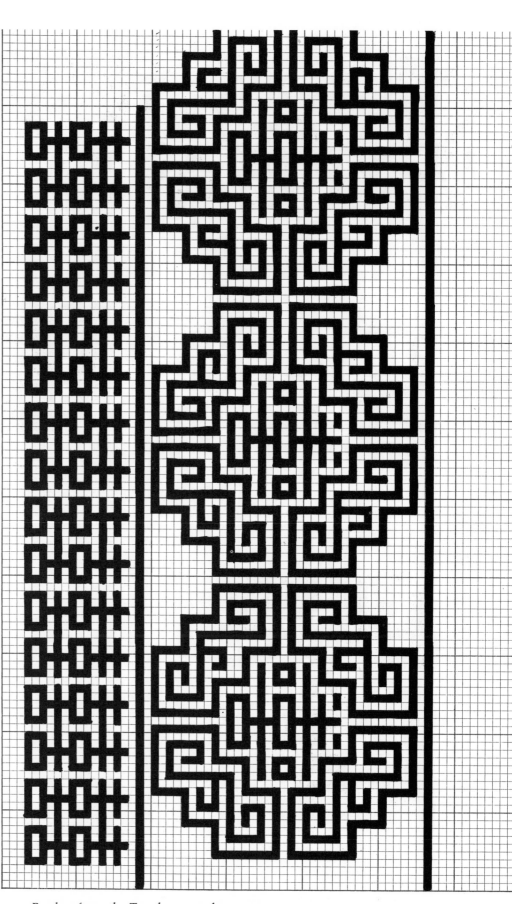

Top

Borders from the Tsonhua sampler

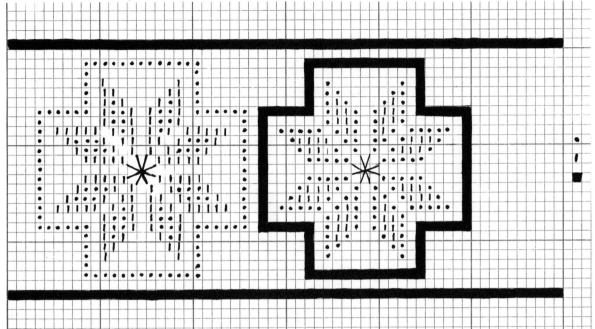

PEACH

- *Light*
ı *Medium*
■ *Dark*

A beautiful border depicted the apricot, which was the symbol of beauty and the fair sex. The emblem of joy was the cherry. The pomegranate meant favorable influences, prosperity and the hope of a large family. Another great favorite was the melon, which has many versions. One was charted in the manner shown on page 27.

Apricot

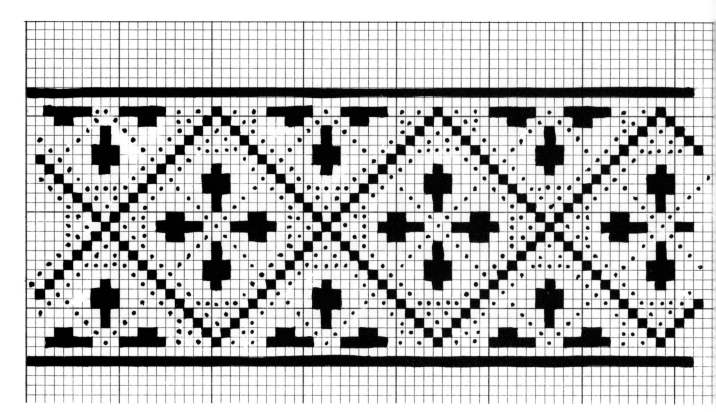

Cherry

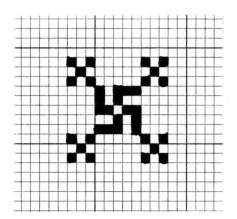

Swastika

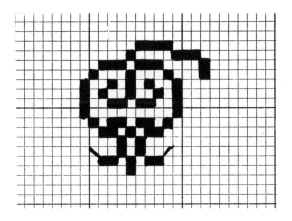

Pomegranate

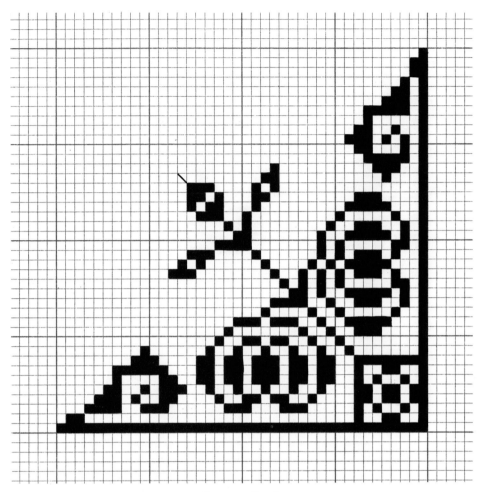

Rinceau Border

The leaves of all the fruits are strongly geometrized. Vines, tendrils and buds occur often. A special and highly developed form of the vine is the stylized rinceau, which forms the border of so many of the strips.

The swastika is an emblem of great antiquity. It has been used throughout the ages by many countries as a symbol of good omen. To the Chinese it was, among other things, Buddha's heart and was the supreme good luck symbol. It was used in very special places.

Insects such as crickets, praying mantises, dragonflies and the like were unknown in these embroideries. Once in a while we find wasps. When used in connection with a monkey, they illustrate a pun.

Rinceau Border

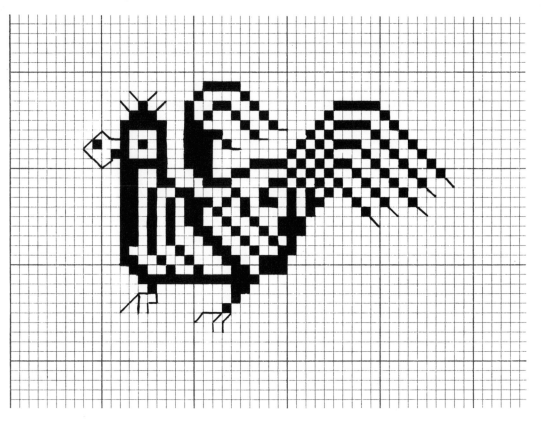

Cock from Tungch'uan sampler—an excellent example

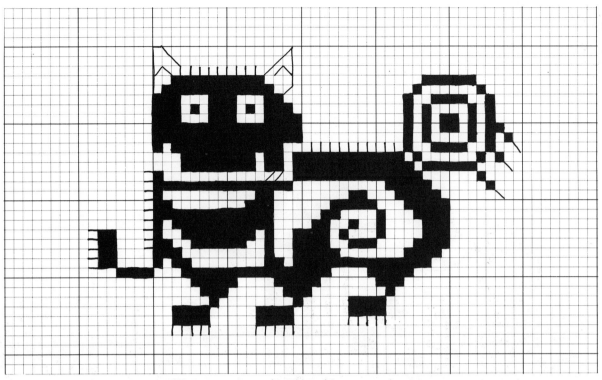

*An unusually fine cat from the Tungch'uan sampler. Note
that its ears are different—this was very typical.*

THE TUNGCH'UAN SAMPLER

Among the many embroideries collected by the late Carl Schuster
during his years in China is a sampler from the town of Tungch'uan
in Yunnan Province. This town is described by Harry Franck as
follows:

The main trail north and south goes through Tungch'uan from east to
west, so that I rode in through the usual large suburb about the West Gate,
as through that outside the East Gate in leaving, before I got into the city
itself. It proved to be a small, compact, perfectly rectangular town of many
fine trees within a good old wall, with a graveyard backed by a temple-
crowned hill, stone tombs climbing far up the sides of the mountains close
on the South that have forced us to come in from the West. They were
high, plump mountains, their slopes more or less velvety deep green in this
rainy season, but still with bare reddish patches, rising all about a place
already 7250 feet above sea level. The city wall of stone and in recent
repair, was about half a mile long and a quarter wide, with a fine grassy

29

Fish and Dragon-gate

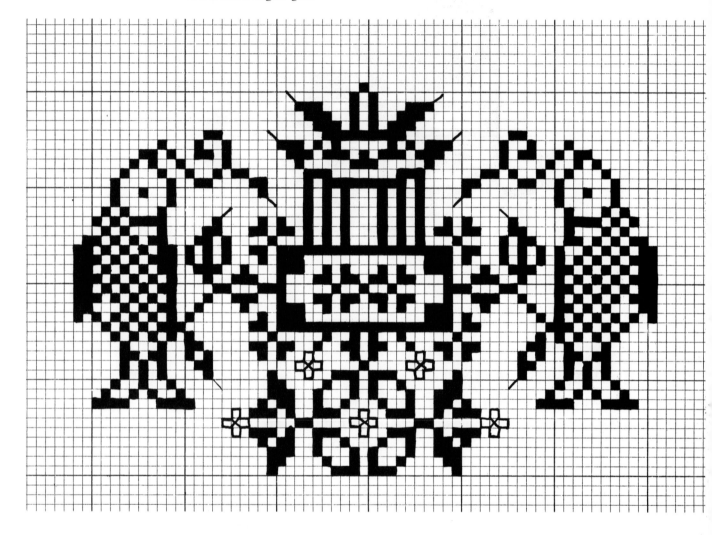

Cat

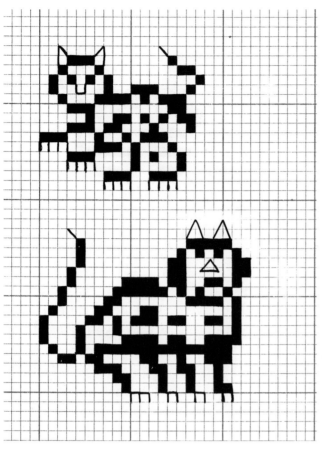

Two Cats

walk around the top, as usual the only good one in town, from which one looked across a great rice plain stretching to mountains with many villages along their skirts. There were the usual mud brick houses, with dull tile roofs, almost so compact as to hide the miserably narrow cobbled streets running among them, and a number of picturesque old temples, especially handsome for their fine old trees and mountain background.

This sampler, with its selection of minor design elements, became a model from which designs could be copied and passed on. It is literally crowded with symbolic motifs. On it are delightful fish, the emblem of wealth, harmony and married joy, the charm to avert all evil.

The cat is a generally good creature to have around, for he is credited with the power to frighten evil spirits away. Thus there are three cats on the sampler in Plate 10.

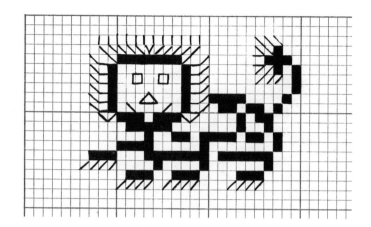

Lion

The noble lion, depicted in the sampler several times, is, of course, the symbol of great courage and bravery. The lions were a very popular motif and more often than not were very like the toy lions made for children. Lions rolling a ball were commonly seen.

One way in which the animals play an important part is their domination of the year in the form of Zodiac animals. Each year is known as the year of some animal; there are twelve in all. They are listed with their Western equivalents. These always appear in the same order:

Rat	*Aries*
Ox	*Taurus*
Tiger	*Gemini*
Hare	*Cancer*
Dragon	*Leo*
Snake	*Virgo*
Horse	*Libra*
Sheep	*Scorpio*
Monkey	*Sagittarius*
Cock	*Capricorn*
Dog	*Aquarius*
Boar	*Pisces*

Because the sequence is unvarying, it sometimes helps to fix with some degree of accuracy the age of a piece of embroidery.

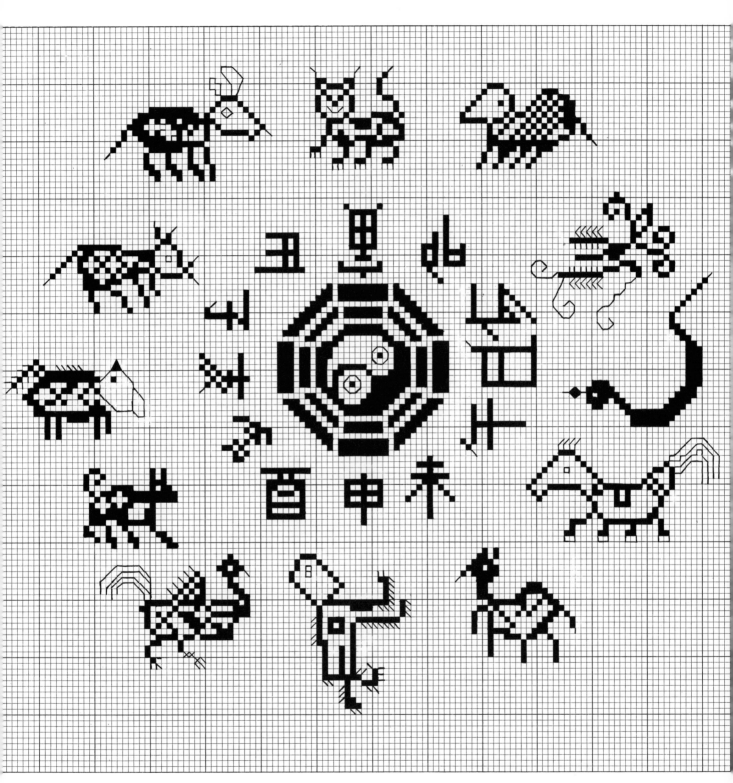

Chinese Zodiac. Note Yin-Yang symbol in the center.
An interesting delineation of the various animals.

Urn of stylized flowers—the one on the left is a Buddha's hand.
A good example of large areas broken up by small motifs.

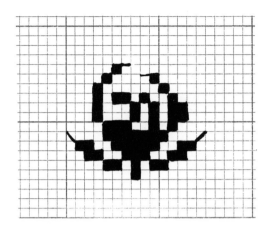

Buddha's Hand

In the Tungch'uan sampler we also find "Buddha's Hand." This is a representation of an inedible fruit, which is very fragrant. It is used, because of its shape, to represent Buddha's hand with the index and little fingers pointing upward. This is considered a most auspicious omen.

A small boy riding a unicorn is shown on the sampler on Plate 10. He holds in his hand a sprig of cassia blossoms, which shows that he will rise to greatness. The unicorn on which he rides is a very good omen; in fact it is the omen of perfect good.

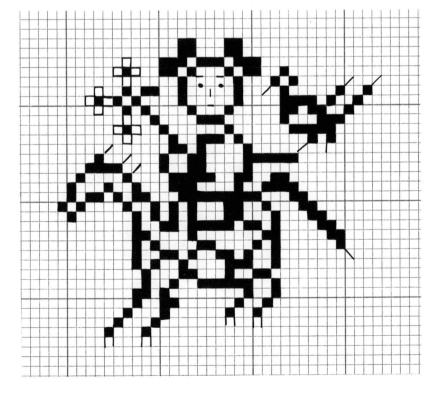

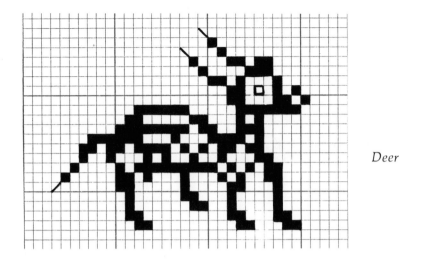

Deer

In these embroideries we often find a deer, which seems to have no special significance. It was probably a common sight for the country folk, who used it as a model. Generally, it has a sprig in its mouth.

The monkey was used almost entirely to illustrate puns and is a familiar figure in the cycle of Chinese fairy tales. It is the symbol of trickery.

The horse, that sturdy animal, the emblem of perseverance, is seen chiefly as a mounted animal in wedding and funeral processions or in

Rat

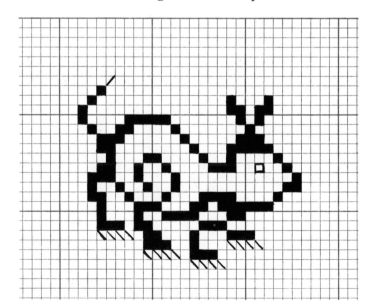

groups showing the triumphal entrance of some important official. Many of the designs involving horses are especially charming.

In Yunnan Province, the rabbit occurs frequently on women's apron tops. Worn as a talisman, it was guaranteed to eat all evil!

Again in Yunnan Province, we find the fish to be a very popular device. Emblem of wealth, bliss and harmony, it too can avert evil. The fish in these embroideries are very naturalistic. Most have feelers like catfish. Almost all fish show the attachment of sprigs of sea grass to their bodies. Sometimes these sprigs protrude from the mouth. The pearl seen quite frequently was considered the product of the fish and is one of the Eight Ordinary Symbols. It is a good sign denoting genius, purity and feminine beauty. The Eight Ordinary Symbols show great variance, but according to Dr. Schuster they are the Pearl, Lozenge, Stone Chime, Rhino's Horn, Mirror, Book, Leaf and Coin.

There are a number of categories of auspicious objects, sometimes eight, sometimes one hundred! Many are associated with Buddhism, some with Taoism; others are secular. They are often confused, and motifs from one group are substituted for those of another.

The flowers of the Chinese rural workers are as unnatural as the phoenix and even more unstable in form. In most cases they identify with the lotus. Sometimes they are shown with their root. The apple blossom is regarded as a symbol of beauty and peace, the chrysanthemum is the symbol of laughter, a life of ease, and it is the national

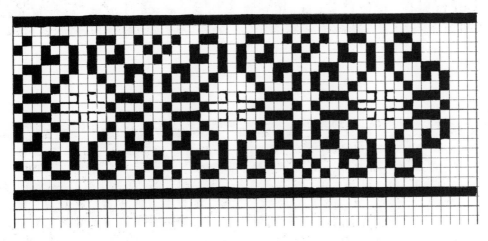

Butterflies

Hollyhock

Butterfly and Double Happiness

Wild Plum

Lotus

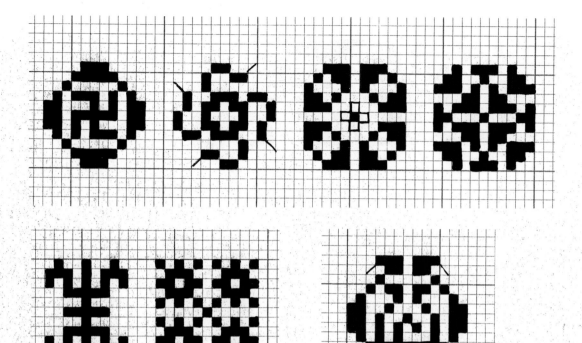

flower. In these embroideries it is highly conventionalized, often to the point of being unrecognizable. The peony stands for love and affection, brightness and masculinity, as well as good fortune.

Chinese characters used decoratively in these designs were longevity, happiness, wealth and good luck. We find them over and over again, often interwoven with one another.

Geometric ornaments such as the rosette, the spiral and the S-curve were used to express a meaning—precisely what is a mystery, lost somewhere in time. Their latent symbolism appears only when they are applied in important positions such as on the bodies of birds or animals or the central diagrams of the radial medallions. Then they are elevated to importance as mystic signs.

When squares are superimposed they become a cosmological symbol very ancient and very widespread. We also find the octagon, the triangle and the eight-pointed star; the significance of these has long since been lost.

39

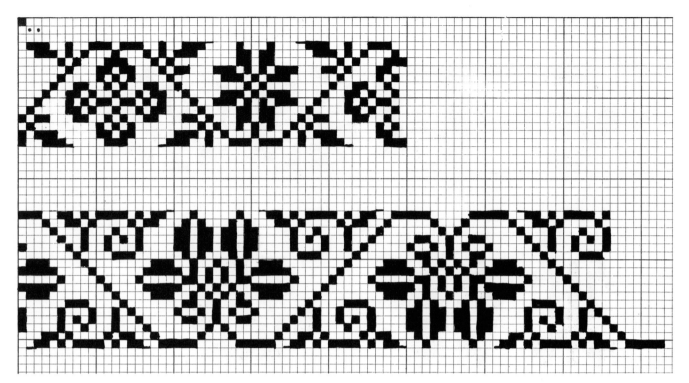

A group of rinceau borders

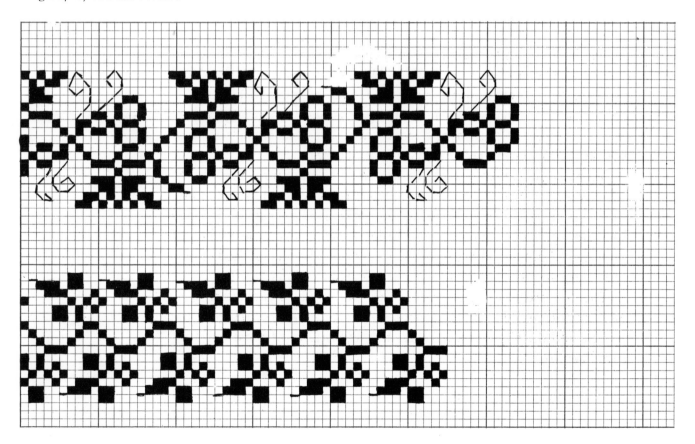

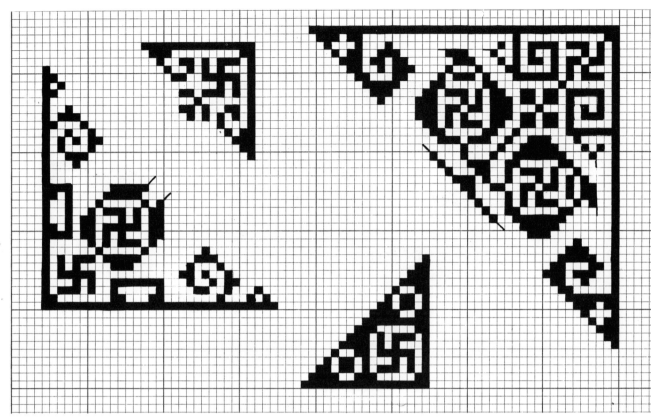

A group of typical corner designs. These are sometimes turned back to back to form another motif.

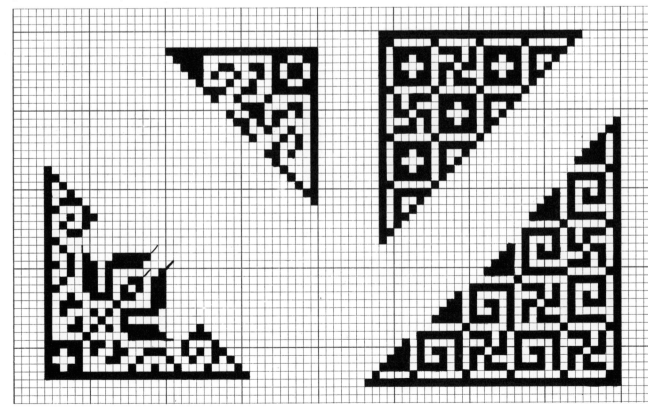

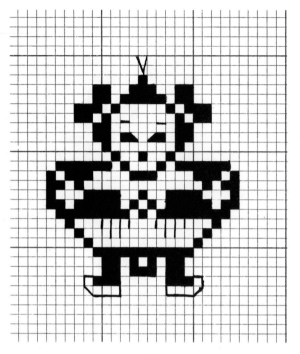
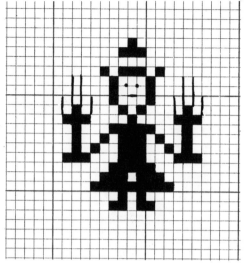

The use of human figures seems to correspond to certain geographical regions; in Szechwan they seem to have their best interpretation. Even here they are greatly denaturalized. The men have thick-soled shoes and caps, either turbans, officials' caps or the common round cap. The women have triangular shoes and bound feet, wear fancy head ornaments and often have striped skirts. These were often used in the designs that were rebuses or fairy tales. One would have to know Chinese very well in order to interpret them correctly. Often even a knowledge of ordinary Chinese culture and language would do no good. The meaning of the symbols appears to be exclusive to the area where they were made and is undoubtedly rooted in local, not necessarily ethnic, Chinese legend and folklore.

It would be remiss not to mention the key or return pattern because it is so frequently found. Called "thunder" by the Chinese, it comes from archaic pictographs which represent thunder clouds. To the country people this has a very special significance—thunder meant rain and rain was essential to a good harvest.

42

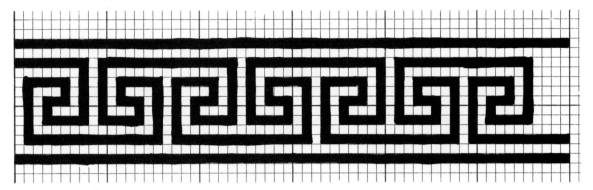

Return

INDIGO DYES

Tu lan tien ch'ing is the very spirit of these embroideries because were it not for indigo there would be none as such! In China, indigo is grown on most of the hill farms. The leaves and stem are cut off and soaked in water. After the water has turned blue, potash is added. Then the mixture is allowed to stand, mellowing, for about two weeks, during which time the indigo is reduced. This solution is used for dyeing the cotton cloth from which much clothing is made and also for the threads which were used in these embroideries. The shade of indigo depends on the age of the mixture and the length of time the material is left in the pot. The older the mixture becomes the lighter the blue that results. A fresh, new pot would produce a blue so dark as to be almost black. When the desired depth of color has been reached, the fabric or thread is sun-dried.

Typical embroideries are the blue on white, but some individualistic workers, chiefly in Yunnan and Hupeh Provinces, use white on blue, a color scheme that is not nearly as effective. In Yunnan, the traditional motifs are sometimes found on red or green cotton backgrounds. In Yunnan Province there is a large concentration of an ethnic group known as the Miaos. They are not truly Chinese, having come from the Far East, and it seems to be from this group that most of the uncharacteristic embroideries come. While the Chinese used mainly cross-stitch, these same Miaos used stitches reminiscent of blackwork.

43

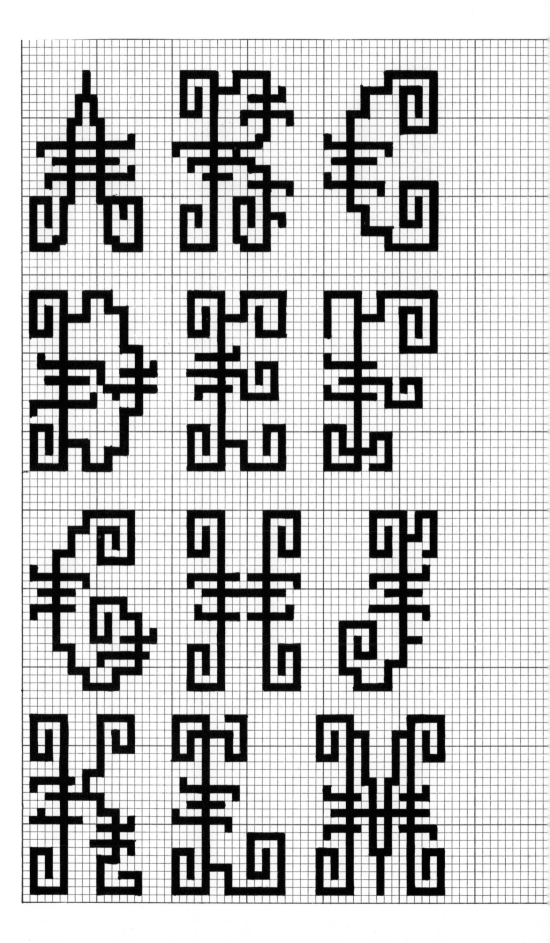

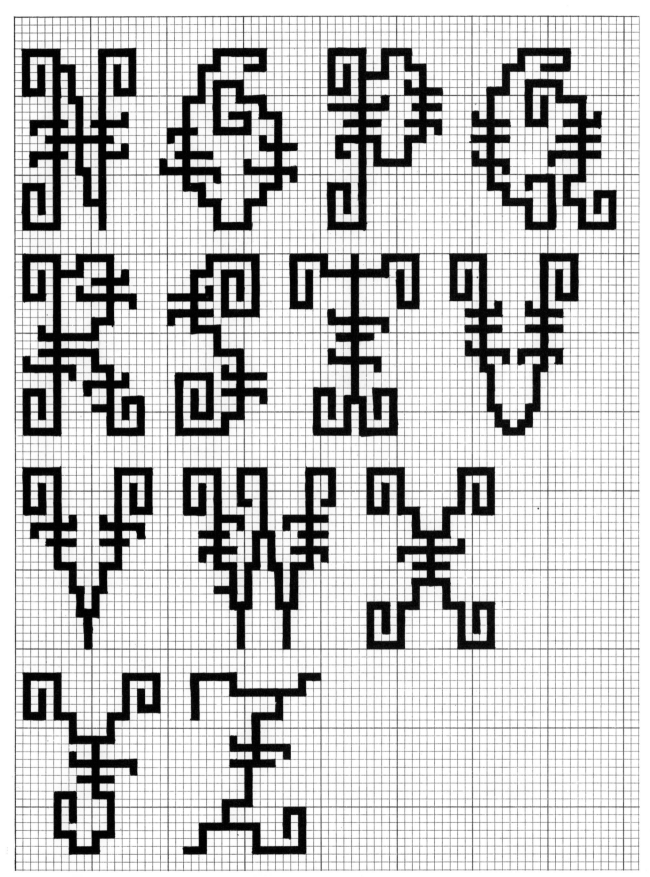

An alphabet in Chinese style for the worker who wants to sign a piece

THE CROSS-STITCH AND THE MATERIALS

In the cross-stitch, a stitch that was practiced in the T'ang Dynasty (618–906 A.D.), the stitches are invariably connected on the back of the material by parallel lines, usually vertical. Generally, three threads of the material are crossed, but it may be up to five. Not infrequently a single piece will show work on more than one thread count! This sometimes corresponds to a difference in the spirit of the designs and suggests that more than one person may have worked on the piece, or perhaps one person at different times of life.

As we have seen, almost without exception, these embroidered pieces are on cotton cloth, handwoven on wooden looms in small village workshops, never in the homes. There is no standardization in the width of these looms. Most pieces vary between 12 and 25 inches in width.

As for the thread used, it is usually hand-twisted cotton, although occasionally accents, such as lips, hair and ribbons, are embroidered in brightly colored silk threads. Once in a while, a piece is hemmed in silk thread, which is apparently preferred for sewing. The hems of these pieces have a distinctive characteristic: they are turned to the right side of the material. This often gives the appearance of an added border.

The cross-stitches are worked in the following manner: Work one half of the stitch from left to right, then the other half from right to left. The needle is passed vertically and the back of the work shows rows of vertical stitches.

These designs may be worked on an even-weave material with cotton embroidery thread. On 25–27 thread count, two strands of six-strand is good. If a coarser material is used, increase the number of strands.

Since canvas is also an even-weave textile, try these designs on 14, 18 or 22 mono canvas. Either tent stitch or cross-stitch may be used to execute them. On a 14-mesh canvas, two strands of yarn cover nicely.

46

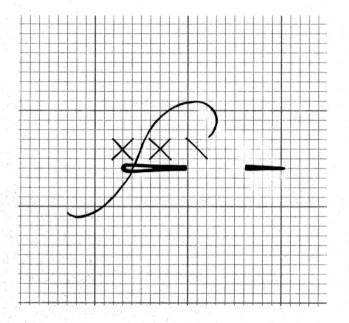

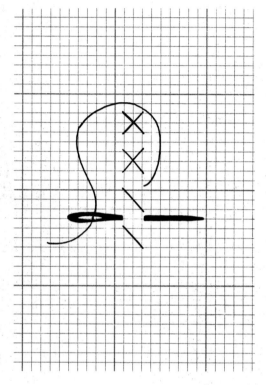

As with any designs of this nature, start at the exact center and work out from that point. The charts are easy to follow once you have become accustomed to reading them, and when you are finished you will have a unique piece of embroidery.

These pieces are great rarities because they were made in inaccessible areas remote from the trading routes and not considered valuable enough to sell. They were completely unknown in the sophisticated artwork of the greatly admired silk embroideries. Except for the perception of a few people like Dr. Schuster and Miranda Packard, these fascinating pieces would be completely lost today.

A very different piece purchased in Nanchiang. This represents a cosmic chess game. The players, each of whom represents one of the four corners of the earth, are different colors. In the petals of the large central flower are Chinese domino pieces. The fish on all four sides represent the oceans surrounding the world. Not too many polychrome pieces were made. These were probably localized in one province. Field Museum of Natural History

50

Cock with a man on his back. Note the similarity of the pattern on the cock's body to that on other illustrated birds and animals. Courtesy Museum of Fine Arts, Boston

This familiar rabbit has been translated from cross-stitch to the canvas medium. All charts may be effectively worked on either linen or canvas.

Mirror cover. Five birds among stylized motifs of the round medallion. Fish border. Courtesy of Museum of Fine Arts, Boston

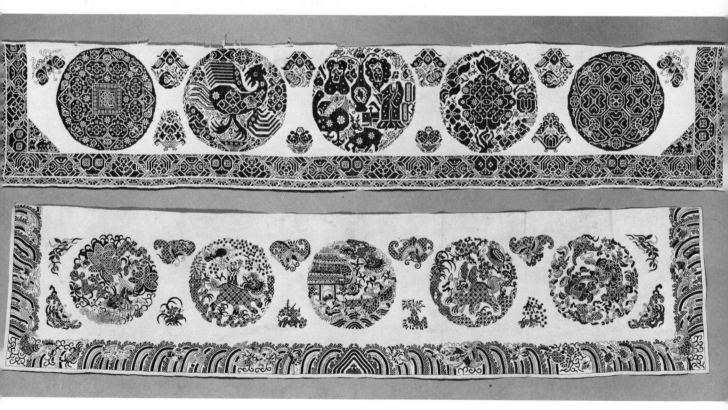

Two bed valances from Pachow, showing ten medallions, each very different from any other. The variety of these medallions is a never-ending surprise. The lower border is especially fine and contains marvelous sea creatures. Field Museum of Natural History

Detail of bed valance, shown on page 53. Very fine birds, butterflies, fish, crab, the famed three-legged toad and assorted insects. The wave border is also exceptionally good. Field Museum of Natural History

54

Plate 1. A small sampler collected by Miranda Packard in Tsonhua. The two little lions are especially good.

Plate 2. A sampler worked by Margaret Lunt from the old ones.

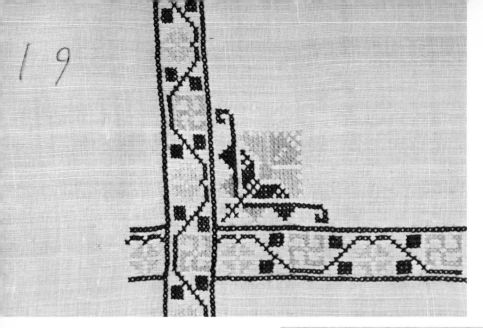

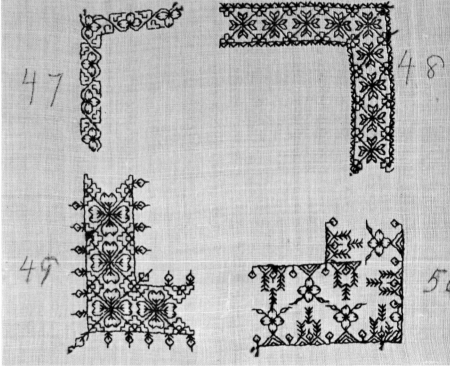

Plate 3. This is a sample—note the number. These samples were sent by missionaries to various groups in this country who took orders for tablecloths, mats, towels and the like. Many so-called missionary pieces are still in use today.

Plates 3–6 show the many types of designs used in the missionary pieces. Although a majority of these were indigo blue on a thin, finely woven white linen, some were stitched in black, some in green and some in yellow.

Plate 4. Excellent rinceau borders, featuring butterflies.

Plate 5. The square mat is a good example of a missionary piece.

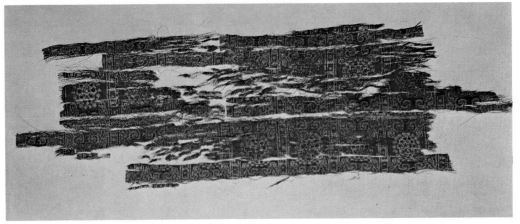

Plate 6. This shows both the front and the back of a piece. The lines on the back are vertical. There are only a few examples where this is not true.

Plate 7. This sash of Su-chiang brocade was produced in Szechwan Province just before or just after the beginning of the T'ang period. It shows the familiar round medallion pattern found in the country embroideries, many of which also come from Szechwan. From The Golden Age of Chinese Art *by Hugh Scott (Rutland, Vt.: Charles E. Tuttle Co.)*

Plate 8. This is a bed valance purchased in Chienchow. It has no medallions, but rather a variety of motifs distributed over the field, more or less in sampler fashion. Especially prominent are a pair of dragon boats in full panoply confronting a flaming jewel. All are done in an attractive, naïve spirit.

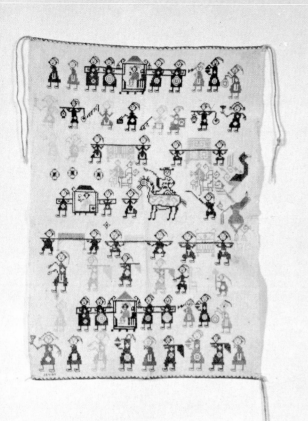

Plate 9. A wedding procession. Note the bride in the sedan chair. Here again we see the use of a few colored silks. This example was bought in Paoning. These treasured pieces passed from mother to daughter and were much used. An old woman, when asked if she had any of these embroideries, replied, "I know what kind you want, they are the kind which you had to copy from a model stitch by stitch. The modern pieces are merely drawn on the cloth and the lines then followed with cross-stitches. With the old kind of work, unless you have a model, you can't do it."

Plate 10. From Tungch'uan in Yunnan Province comes this very detailed sampler with its myriad of units and border designs. Dr. Schuster considered this sampler one of the best he uncovered and it has many charming motifs.

Detail of bed valance, shown on page 53. Vase at center with fruit at left and a leaf at right, both of which have small figures within. The cock at the left is excellent as is the deer at center bottom. Field Museum of Natural History

55

56

Motif featuring an amulet or locket, along with small figures, beasties and fish.
The amulet or locket was to lock the soul in the body. Field Museum of Natural
History

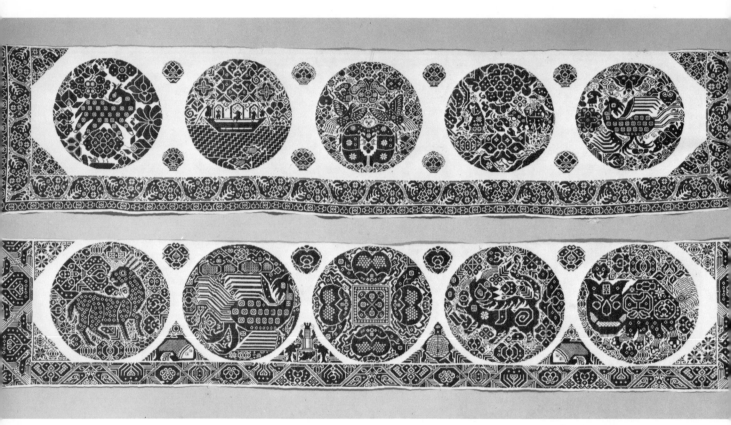

The most interesting of the medallions shown here is the boat. Not all boats were dragon boats; this one depicts man's journey from birth to death. Opposite is a chart of the rabbit in the upper left medallion. Field Museum of Natural History

58

The bed valance, of which this is one medallion, measures 78½ inches by 13¼ inches. The length may vary somewhat, but these are quite standard measurements. Courtesy Museum of Fine Arts, Boston

A friendly rabbit playing among stylized flowers, one version of a favorite theme. The rabbit's head is always turned as he watches over his shoulder. Field Museum of Natural History

An unusually stylized medallion. Most have more action and only a few are mirror images as this one is. Courtesy Museum of Fine Arts, Boston

A "most happy fella" with two birds of excellent omen; note the swastikas on their bodies. The whole medallion has a gay air. Field Museum of Natural History

Another version of the rabbit, that animal of auspicious omen. There is much well-thought-out detail in the background. Field Museum of Natural History

This medallion shows a man standing on a mythical beastie. Despite the stylized motifs surrounding the central figures, there is plenty of movement. Field Museum of Natural History

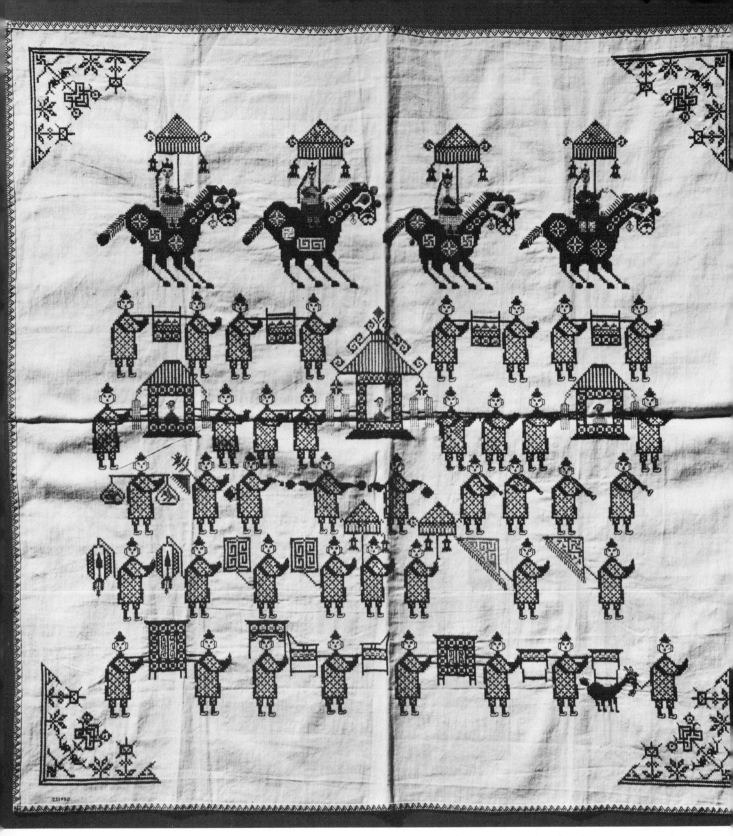

A magnificent procession of dignitaries. There is great detail. The canopies and banners are beautifully depicted and even the horses have emblems of good omen on their bodies. Note the goat that leads the line of march. Field Museum of Natural History

Another version of the domestic cock, this time with two riding figures. One figure boasts two auspicious symbols on his robe, the swastika and the longevity symbol. The other has coins, a symbol of wealth and position. There is a rather interesting border treatment. Field Museum of Natural History

Detail of the procession on preceding page. Note the sway-backed horses. All the horses in these embroideries seem to have the same affliction! Field Museum of Natural History

A pleasing medallion of stylized motifs. The four flower baskets are each quite individual, fine designs in themselves. Field Museum of Natural History

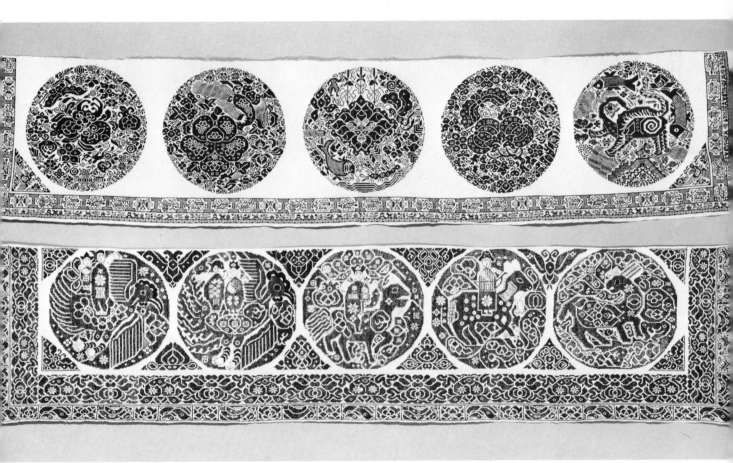

A good pair of bed hangings, showing a great variety of medallions, both stylized and pictorial. Both styles seem to have been favored by the makers; one type does not seem to have been preferred over the other. Field Museum of Natural History

Detail of bed hanging on preceding page. The cat in the fish pond is so bemused by the fish that his head is nearly upside down! Field Museum of Natural History

77

This is a very fine beastie riding proudly on two clouds. This medallion is the representation of a myth. Field Museum of Natural History

A very exciting valance with all five medallions of equal strength. All feature some striking bird or animal and all tell a story. The rosettes on the bodies of the birds and animals are mystic signs of great omen. Field Museum of Natural History

Fine square cloth with well-executed stitches in the darkest of indigos. Field Museum of Natural History

Rabbit turning his head away from a small bird, from valance on page 80. Note similarity to lower right motif on page 88. Apparently the bird and rabbit were either a story or a rebus and the background could be filled in as the maker chose without harming the story line. Field Museum of Natural History

This piece shows a wedding procession with banners, lanterns and the bride
and groom in sedan chairs. It has been photographed to show the typical vertical
stitches left on the back of the work. Copper coins are attached at the upper
corners. Field Museum of Natural History

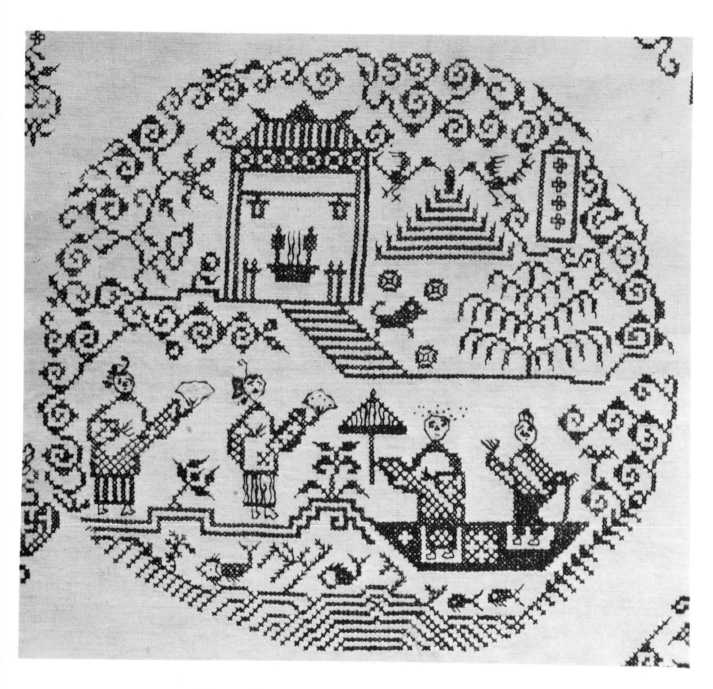

This medallion tells a story of a household getting ready for honored guests.
Field Museum of Natural History

A wedding scene in which each detail corresponds to a feature of the ceremony in real life. A fine example of a pictorial motif as used in the designs. Field Museum of Natural History

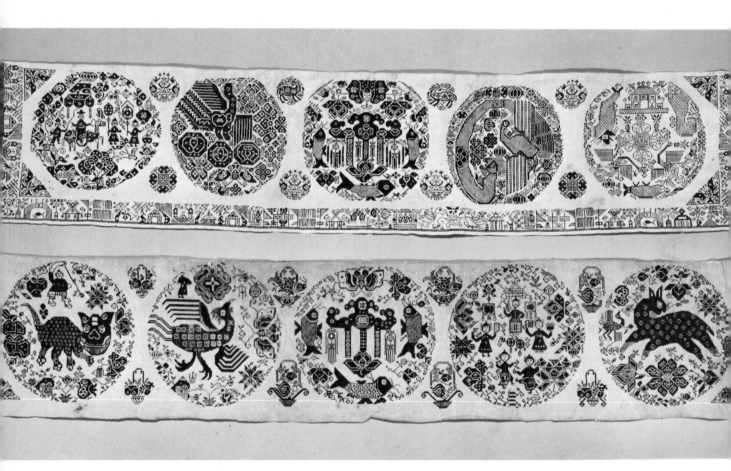

Every medallion of the ten shown merits study. Each is very different and all are extremely well executed, with fine, even stitches. Field Museum of Natural History

This is a domestic cock, which is usually depicted with a riding figure (this one is quite small). Fish in gate and flower basket at lower right are good motifs. *Field Museum of Natural History*

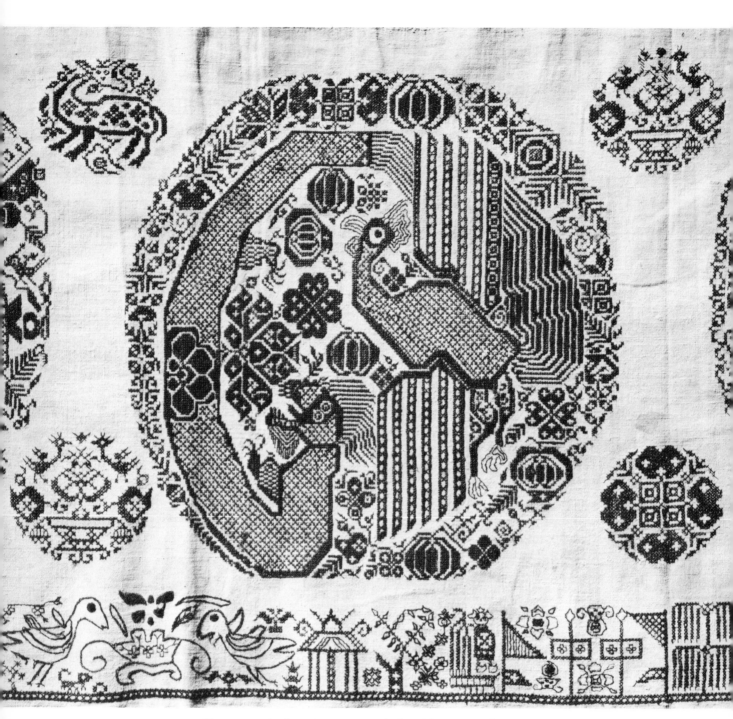

Dragon and phoenix, two symbols of great good omen, dominate the medallion. The small flower baskets with birds are excellent. The deer with reversed head holding a sprig in its mouth is a standard motif of the Chinese decorative style. The border is not as good as the rest of the piece, being rather skimpy. From valance on page 88. Field Museum of Natural History

Excellent butterflies, both without and within the central square. One of the few mirror images, and here the count is not exactly the same on the four sides. Textile Museum, Washington, D.C.

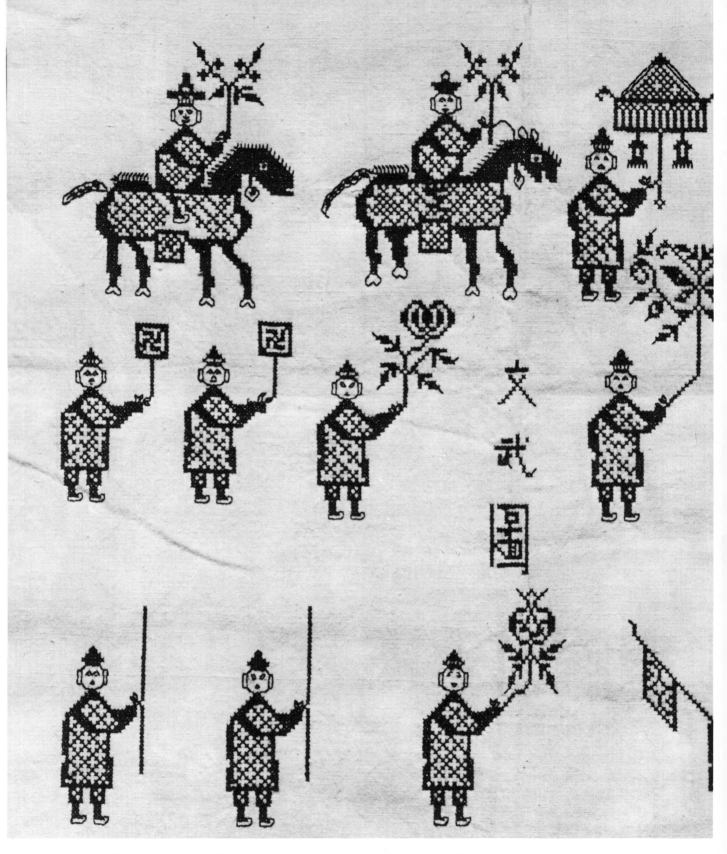

Still another procession. This time the riders are carrying sprigs. Their attendants are also carrying sprigs and flowers. Two are bearing swastikas. Field Museum of Natural History

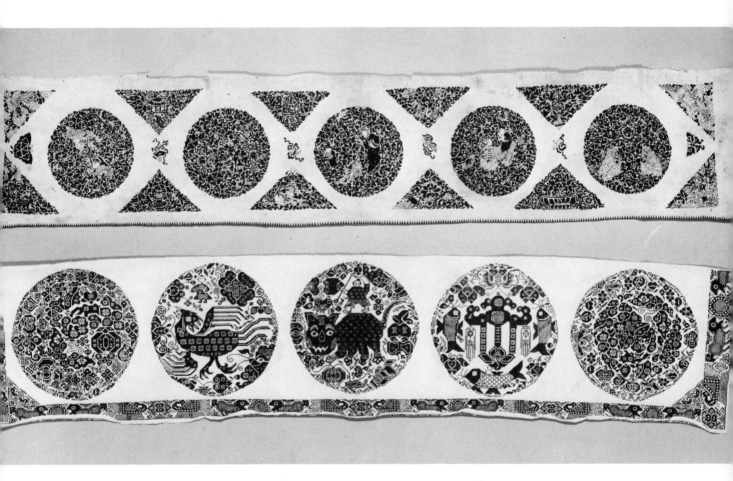

Two different types of central medallions are shown here. The top ones are
so densely executed that the motifs are nearly lost. The lower ones are of the
storytelling type. Field Museum of Natural History

A fine example of a rabbit medallion

A very literal rendition of an elaborate wedding procession. This was a favorite subject for the embroideress; weddings and funerals were very much a part of family life and the concept of the family was at the heart of rural China. Field Museum of Natural History

Procession featuring a dignitary riding on a sway-backed horse. A sway-backed horse is seen so often it must have some significance! This one has small medallions within its body, very carefully done. Human figures bear pennants and canopies; beneath all are the Five Poisons, a talisman to ward off evil. Field Museum of Natural History

Child's dress, full of a spirit of play as well as good omens for the child's future. Many of these jackets feature a locket or amulet. These were substitutes for actual lockets of silver. Such lockets are called chia so *("a hundred family locks"), alluding to the supposition that the locket is paid for with the contributions from a hundred families whose goodwill toward the child is thus concentrated in the amulet. Thus, the child's life is securely "locked" in his body, and he is assured of long life, happiness and honor. Field Museum of Natural History*

This piece was purchased in Loch'in for 70¢. Whether this was high or low is not known, but Dr. Schuster thought it worthy of note. Medallion 4 is especially good, having a boy in a dragon-gate with fish in water. The border is a very good rinceau and there is a good variety of fillers. Field Museum of Natural History

98

This piece is somewhat unusual in that there are two small motifs in magenta
silk thread while the rest is in the usual dark blue cross-stitch. Probably the silk
was a gift to the maker, who could not resist using it. There is a border of
auspicious symbols along one end. *Field Museum of Natural History*

A child's vest, showing the dragon-gate without the usual figure. A dainty border surrounds the design. Field Museum of Natural History

*White on blue. An unusual motif in that it does not follow the same conforma-
tion as the majority of these medallions. The upper tree is an unusual shape.
Grapevine or arbor is in upper right. This mirror cover is from Tungch'uan.
Field Museum of Natural History*

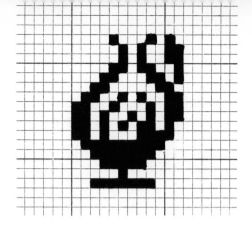

BIBLIOGRAPHY

SCHUSTER, DR. CARL. Unpublished notes, edited by Muriel Baker. Chicago, Illinois: Field Museum of Natural History, 1975.

SCHUSTER, DR. CARL. *Asia Magazine*, January 1937.

SCHUSTER, DR. CARL. *Embroidery.* September 1935.

SCHUSTER, DR. CARL. *The Bird Motif in Chinese Peasant Embroidery.* Heidelberg, Germany, 1936.

PACKARD, MIRANDA. Unpublished notes, edited by Margaret Lunt, 1975.

FRANCK, HARRY A. *Roving Through Southern China.* New York: Century Company, 1925.

PRIP-MOLLER, ANTONETTE. *Gamle Kinesiske Korsting.* Copenhagen, Denmark: Horst & Sons Forlag, n.d.

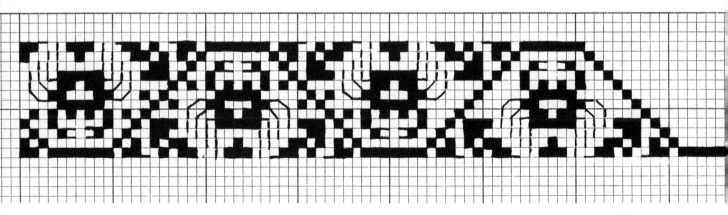

Crab border